WHAT MAKES AN OCEAN WAVE?

Questions and Answers
About Oceans and Ocean Life

BY MELVIN AND GILDA BERGER

ILLUSTRATED BY JOHN RICE

SCHOLASTIC REFERENCE

CONTENTS

KEY TO ABBREVIATIONS

cm = centimeter/centimetre
cm² = square centimeter/centimetre
kg = kilogram
km = kilometer/kilometre
km² = square kilometer/kilometre
m = meter/metre
mm = millimeter/millimetre
t = tonne

Text copyright © 2000 by Melvin and Gilda Berger
Illustrations copyright © 2000 by John Rice
All rights reserved. Published by Scholastic Inc.
SCHOLASTIC and associated logos are trademarks and/or registered trademarks of Scholastic Inc.

No part of this publication may be reproduced, or stored in a retrieval system, or transmitted in any form or by any means, electronic, mechanical, photocopying, recording, or otherwise, without written permission of the publisher. For information regarding permission, write to Scholastic Inc., Attention: Permissions Department, 555 Broadway, New York, NY 10012.

Library of Congress Cataloging-in-Publication Data

Berger, Melvin.
    What makes an ocean wave? : questions and answers about oceans / by Melvin Berger and
    Gilda Berger; illustrated by John Rice.
        p.   cm.—(Scholastic question and answer series)
    Includes index.
    Summary: Provides information about various aspects of the world's oceans—waves, tides, the food chain, marine creatures, coastlines and more.
    1. Oceanography—Miscellanea—Juvenile literature. 2. Marine ecology—Miscellanea—Juvenile literature. 3. Ocean—Miscellanea—Juvenile literature. [1. Ocean—Miscellanea. 2. Marine animals—Miscellanea. 3. Questions and answers] I. Berger, Gilda. II. Rice, John, illus. III. Title. IV. Series: Berger, Melvin. Scholastic question and answer series.
GC21.5 .B48 2000 551.46—dc21 99-041771 CIP AC

ISBN 0-439-09588-3 (pob); ISBN 0-439-14882-0 (pb)

Book design by David Saylor and Nancy Sabato

10 9 8 7 6   03 04

Printed in the U.S.A.   08
First trade printing, March 2001

Expert Reader: Lisa Mielke
Assistant Director of Education
New York Aquarium
Brooklyn, NY

For Betty and Dan, with whom we share our love of the ocean — from Provincetown to the Hamptons
— M. AND G. BERGER

To all the children whose love of nature creates an insatiable need to know the secrets hidden in the oceans of the world . . . and also to Wendy
— J. RICE

INTRODUCTION

Suppose you could look down at Earth from space. You would see a planet that looks like it is almost all water. That's because the oceans of the world cover almost three-quarters of Earth's surface!

Life on Earth started in the ocean. Today, millions of different plants and animals live in these vast bodies of water. Each one—from the tiniest shrimp to the greatest blue whale— is an important link in the giant web of life in the sea.

Did you know that we could not survive without the oceans? Water that evaporates from the oceans falls as rain and gives us the water we use for drinking, washing, and cooking. Fish and other seafood that we eat come from the oceans. Oceans spread the sun's warmth around the globe. And from the oceans, too, we get such valuable resources as oil, gas, and minerals.

All of us depend on the oceans. More and more, we are coming to understand that the future of the oceans depends on us. One way or another, our future and the future of the oceans are linked. Let's read and find out why.

Melvin Berger   Gilda Berger

OCEAN WATERS

What makes an ocean wave?

The wind blowing across the water. The harder the wind blows, the bigger the wave. Waves can also come from underwater volcanoes or earthquakes. But wind-driven waves are most common.

Does ocean water move forward?

No—even though it looks that way. A wave is made up of many tiny bits of water. Each bit makes a little circle and returns to its starting point.

Watch a gull sitting on the water as a wave passes. You'll see it bob up and down. But both the gull and the water stay in the same place.

You can try this out. Tie a long string to a doorknob. Stretch it out and shake the free end up and down. You'll see the waves pass through the string—but the string itself does not move forward.

Why do waves break near shore?

Because the bottom of the wave begins to drag on the shallow ocean floor. That slows down the lower part of the wave. But the top keeps going until it topples over, which makes the wave break. The breaking wave tosses water, as well as sand and rocks from the ocean bottom, onto the beach. A powerful wave can pick up and fling rocks that weigh more than 100 pounds (45 kg)! Sand and rocks that the waves throw can cut caves or wear away cliffs along the shore.

Herring gulls

Least sandpipers

How do you measure the height of a wave?

From the highest point of the wave, called the crest, to the lowest point, called the trough. The wind pushes the water up, making the crest. Then gravity pulls it down, to create the trough, the valley between the two crests. The height of a wave is the distance from crest to trough.

How high was the highest ocean wave on record?

About 112 feet (34 m), or higher than a 10-story building! The wave was measured in 1933 by sailors on the American tanker USS *Ramapo* during a severe windstorm in the Pacific Ocean.

Most ocean waves are less than 12 feet (3.7 m) high and 25-foot (7.6 m) waves are rare. So you can just imagine how this giant wave scared the sailors!

Are waves dangerous?

Sometimes. Big waves can capsize or wreck ships at sea, especially in storms. In June 1968, the tanker *World Glory* was broken in half by 100-foot (30.5 m) waves. Surfers who try to ride very high waves run the risk of being crushed and drowned if they fall off their surfboards.

What are tsunamis?

Giant waves. Tsunamis, sometimes called tidal waves, come from earthquakes and erupting volcanoes under the sea. The energy from the quakes and volcanoes causes huge waves to travel across thousands of miles of ocean. The waves eventually smash into the shore, where they cause dreadful damage.

How many oceans are there on Earth?

Four—the Pacific, Atlantic, Indian, and Arctic. But look closely at a map and you'll see that the oceans flow into one another. So, in a way, there is just one vast world ocean.

The oceans cover about three-fourths of the earth's surface and contain 97 percent of the world's water. If the ocean water were spread evenly over the entire surface of the earth, the water would be about 2 miles (3.2 km) deep!

Are oceans, seas, gulfs, and bays the same or different?

Different. Oceans are huge bodies of water that separate continents. Seas are smaller than oceans and are partly or completely encircled by land—even though people sometimes say "seas" when they mean oceans. Gulfs are parts of oceans or seas that extend into the land. And bays are like gulfs, only smaller.

Which is the largest ocean?

The Pacific. It covers about 70 million square miles (181 million km²). That's nearly half of the world's oceans. In fact, the Pacific Ocean is larger than all the land surfaces of the earth put together!

What's under the oceans?

Plains, hills, mountains, valleys, and trenches. From the edge of the continents, the land forms a gently sloping underwater ledge, called the continental shelf. Its average width is about 47 miles (76 km).

At the edge of the continental shelf, the land drops steeply. Known as the continental slope, it extends out another 60 miles (97 km).

At the bottom of the slope is the continental rise, a slightly higher area that stretches about 600 miles (1,000 km). Beyond the continental rise is the vast ocean floor, with its deep, steep trenches.

Oceans of the World

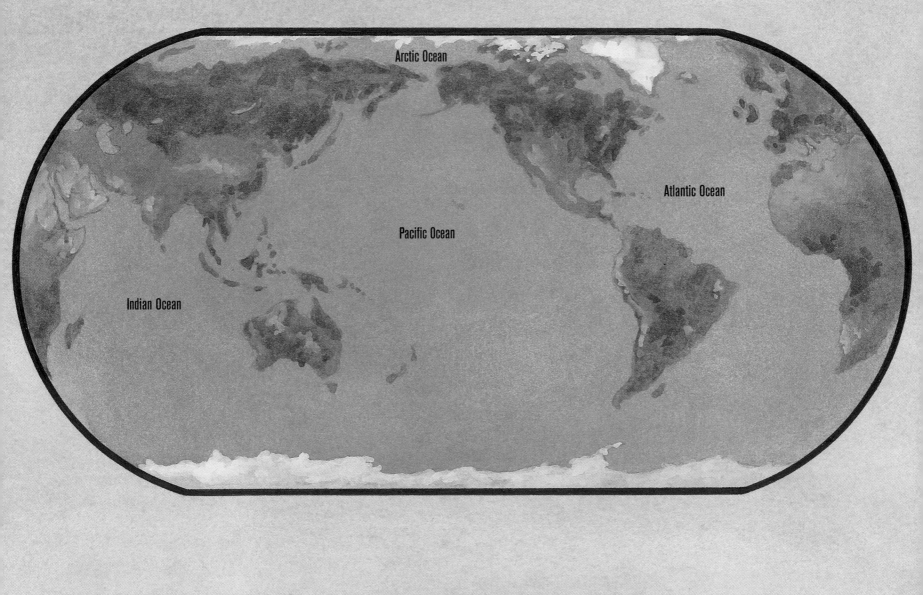

Arctic Ocean

Atlantic Ocean

Pacific Ocean

Indian Ocean

How deep is the ocean?

About 2.3 miles (3.7 km) on average. In 1995, scientists found the deepest known spot in the ocean—6.85 miles (11 km) below the surface—at the bottom of the Marianas Trench in the Pacific Ocean. If you dropped a heavy rock into the water over this spot, it would take more than an hour to reach the bottom!

Is ocean water heavy?

It sure is. In fact, the deeper you dive into ocean water, the more weight, or pressure, you feel. Animals and plants that live deep in the ocean are used to this pressure. But people are not. That's why people need special diving suits or submarines to explore the ocean depths.

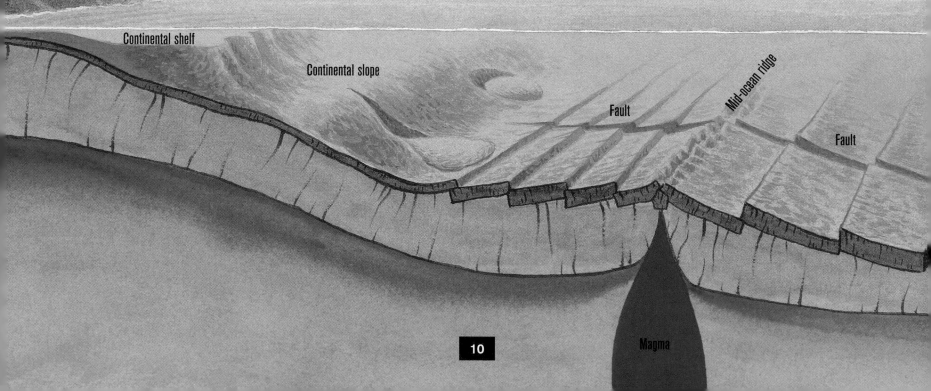

Continental shelf

Continental slope

Fault

Mid-ocean ridge

Fault

Magma

What is the pressure at the bottom of the ocean?

Almost 400 times the pressure at the surface. At the average depth of 2.3 miles (3.7 km), the pressure is 5,454 pounds per square inch (2,474 kg per 6.5 cm²). Compare this with the 14.7 pounds per square inch (6.7 kg per 6.5 cm²) at the surface! Suppose you took a block of wood to the bottom of the ocean. The pressure would squeeze the wood into a block half its size!

How deep can you go?

Only a few hundred feet (meters) in a scuba outfit or diving suit connected to a surface source of air. But you can go much deeper in an underwater craft, called a submersible. This specially-built submarine protects people from high pressure underwater.

One submersible, the *Trieste*, went to the bottom of the Marianas Trench. The trip took nearly five hours. If you ever go there, remember to bring your lunch!

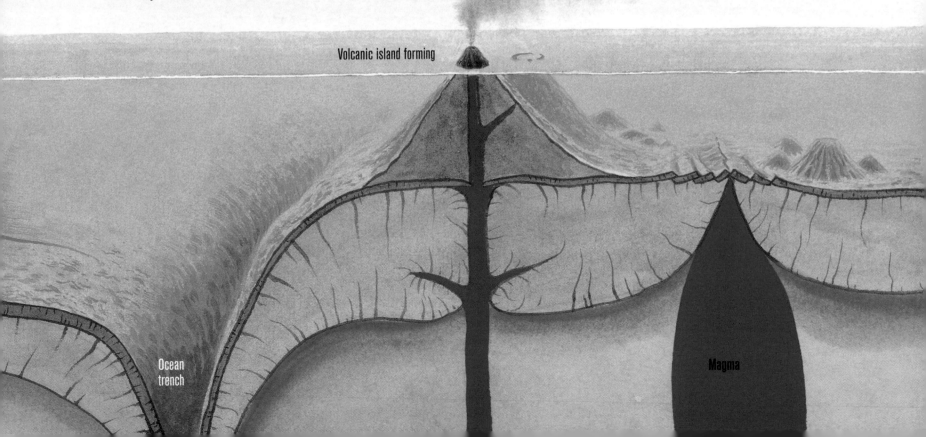

Volcanic island forming

Ocean trench

Magma

Are tides the same as waves?

Yes and no. Tides are slow, regular waves. But they are caused by gravity, not the wind.

　The best places to see tides are along ocean coasts. The water rises between 2 and 10 feet (0.6 and 3 m) at high tide. The highest tides are found in the funnel-shaped Bay of Fundy in southeast Canada. They rise as much as 50 feet (15 m) above low tide!

What causes high tides?

Mainly the moon. When the moon is overhead, its gravity pulls on the ocean waters directly below. This causes a high tide. As the earth turns, you usually get high tide at each place on the ocean twice a day. From one high tide to the next takes about $12\frac{1}{2}$ hours.

　Tides are also caused by the constant pull of the sun on Earth. But because the moon is so much closer to Earth, its pull is more than twice as strong as the sun's pull.

When do the highest and lowest tides occur?

Twice a month. The highest of the high tides occurs when the sun, moon, and Earth are in a line. These are called spring tides, even though they have nothing to do with the season of the year. Spring tides come at both the new moon and the full moon, when both the moon and sun are pulling ocean water in the same direction.

　When the moon and sun are at right angles to each other, the pull of gravity is weaker. The lowest high tides, called neap tides, occur halfway between a new and full moon.

Where does the water go during low tide?

It moves to another place in the ocean. The bulge of the water makes it high tide there. The water doesn't disappear. It just goes somewhere else.

▲ High Tide

▼ Low Tide

Northern fulmars

What are ocean currents?

Rivers of water flowing through the ocean. Currents are mainly due to steady winds blowing on the ocean's surface. But other forces, such as heat and gravity, also play a part. Currents flow clockwise north of the equator and in the opposite direction south of the equator.

Currents also flow up and down within the water. Cold-water currents come from the polar regions. They are heavier than warm water, so they sink and slowly flow toward the equator. Warm-water currents move more quickly and higher in the water. They flow from the equator toward the poles to replace the sinking cold water.

Do ocean currents affect climate?

Indeed they do. For example, the Gulf Stream is one of the strongest and warmest currents. It starts at the Gulf of Mexico and flows northeast across the Atlantic Ocean, bringing mild weather to parts of Europe. People in London, England, have much the same climate as New Yorkers, even though they live much farther north.

Why is the ocean blue?

Because of the sun. Sunlight is made up of light of all colors. The tiny bits of water bounce back the blue rays more than any of the others, making the water *look* blue. Pure ocean water is really colorless. You can see this for yourself if you look at a glass of seawater!

Does ocean water sometimes take on different colors?

Yes. Ocean water looks green when the yellow of tiny floating plants in the water mixes in with the blue. The Red Sea, between the Arabian peninsula and Africa, is red because it is filled with microscopic plants that give the water a red color. And the Yellow Sea, between China and North and South Korea, is colored by huge amounts of yellow sand dropped there by flowing rivers.

Is the Dead Sea really dead?

Yes, except for a few plants and even fewer animals. The water in the Dead Sea, between Israel and Jordan, has nine times more salt than ocean water, making life there almost impossible. Only tourists enjoy splashing around in these mineral-rich waters!

What makes ocean water salty?

Rivers flowing into the ocean. As freshwater rivers flow across the land they pick up salts from soil and rock. Sooner or later, the rivers flow into the ocean where they drop the salts. When ocean water evaporates, the salt remains in the ocean. The most common salt in seawater is sodium chloride, the kind you sprinkle on your food.

How do we get salt from the sea?

We let ocean water evaporate, or dry up. To do this, workers pump the water into small ponds. Heat from the sun dries up the water. It becomes water vapor, an invisible gas that mixes with the air. The salt that remains is then scooped up and made ready for use.

Can we get fresh water from salt water?

Yes, we can. As the sun warms the ocean, some fresh water evaporates in the form of water vapor, leaving the salt behind. In time, the water vapor in the air changes back into liquid water and falls as freshwater rain or snow. Some rain and snow fall on lakes or rivers, and soak down into underground pools, giving us fresh water for drinking, cooking, and washing.

Today, more than 4,000 factories around the world make fresh water from ocean water. About half are in the Middle East, an area of vast deserts and little rainfall.

Evaporating ponds

A marine biology laboratory

What other natural resources come from the ocean?

Oil, among other substances. About one-fourth of the world's oil comes from offshore wells sunk deep under the ocean floor. From the ocean bottom we also get sand and gravel that workers add to cement to make concrete. And from seawater we get manganese, used to harden steel, and bromine, needed to make photographic film.

Of the 92 natural elements, scientists have found around 70 dissolved in seawater. Also, tons of diamonds, gold, copper, iron, and zinc rest on the ocean floor. There's only one problem. How can we get these resources out at a low cost?

Who explores the ocean?

Scientists called oceanographers. Physical oceanographers study the ocean's waves, tides, currents, and the interaction between the ocean and the atmosphere. Chemical oceanographers test ocean water for saltiness and for other compounds and minerals. Marine geologists probe the formation and makeup of the ocean floor. And marine biologists learn about life in the sea, from the tiniest plants and animals to the largest fish and mammals.

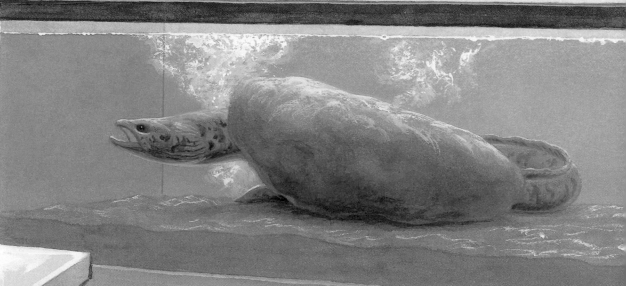

LIFE IN THE OCEAN

Where do you find most life in the ocean?

In the top layer, or "sunlight" zone. Even though it makes up just a small part of the ocean, about 90 percent of all ocean plants and animals live here. On average, the top zone goes down only about 600 feet (180 m). That's as far as the sun's light can reach.

What form of life is most common in the sunlight zone?

Tiny plants and animals called plankton. Plankton are divided into two kinds. The smaller are plant plankton, or phytoplankton. Slightly larger are animal plankton, known as zooplankton. Phytoplankton are the bottom of the food chain in the ocean.

What is the ocean's food chain?

A grouping of living things in the ocean in which each type of living thing feeds on the one below it on the chain. At the bottom of the food chain are microscopic phytoplankton, which use sunlight and minerals in the water to grow. Zooplankton eat phytoplankton. Many ocean animals, including fish and some kinds of whales, feed on zooplankton. The fish, in turn, are eaten by other fish.

When all these animals die, they become food for bacteria, which add minerals to the water. Rising currents carry the minerals up to the sunlight zone where phytoplankton use them to grow and start the food chain in the ocean all over again.

Why else are plankton important?

They produce oxygen. Some of the oxygen gas that plankton make dissolves in the water. But much escapes into the air and becomes the oxygen that humans breathe.

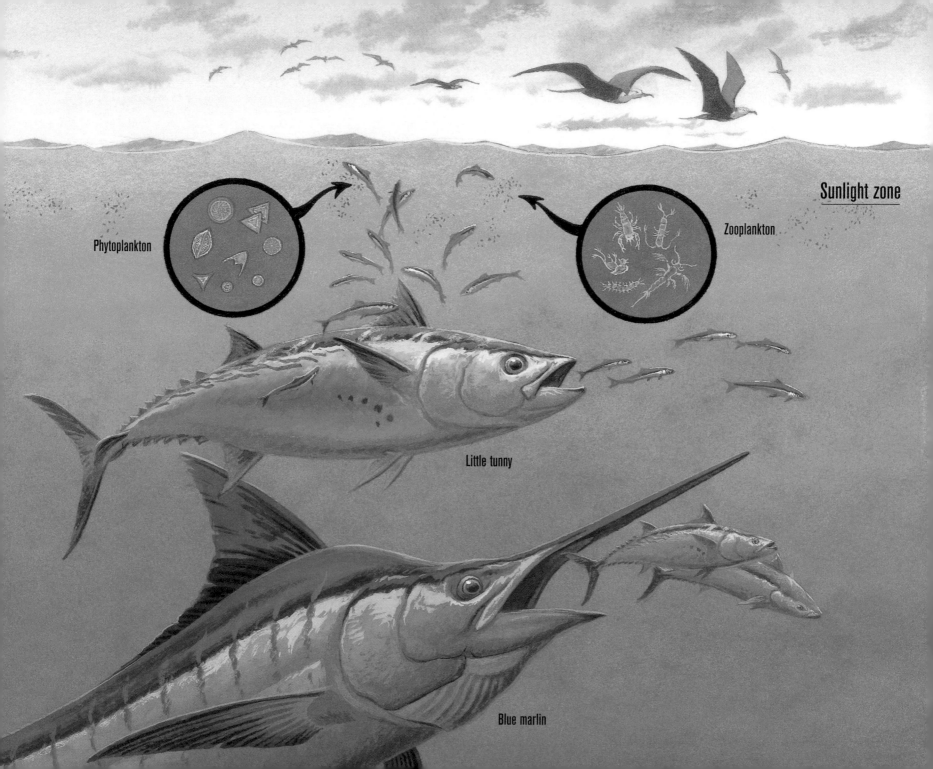

Phytoplankton

Zooplankton

Sunlight zone

Little tunny

Blue marlin

How do humans affect life in the ocean?

Often, they catch or kill too many sea creatures. Overfishing the ocean cuts both the number of sea creatures and the number of species. Take the blue whale, for example. Once there were more than 200,000 blue whales in the seas. Today, because of heavy hunting, only about 14,000 remain.

Pollution also affects life in the ocean. Oil spills can sicken and kill many sea animals. More than 300,000 seabirds died as a result of a single oil spill off the coast of Alaska in 1989.

Which are the most widespread plant plankton?

Diatoms. They make up more than half of all the phytoplankton in the ocean. Yet, most of these drifting specks are less than $\frac{1}{25}$ of an inch (1 mm) long. Their jewel-like shells shimmer in the water. Under a microscope, they look like tiny flashing needles, anchors, bracelets, or golf tees.

What is the most important animal plankton?

Krill. This zooplankton is a valuable food for whales and many other ocean animals.

A krill, which looks like a tiny shrimp, has a great way of protecting itself. When threatened, the krill jumps out of its shell. The creature goes one way and its empty shell floats off in another direction. Often, the enemy chases the shell—and the krill escapes without harm!

Are any plankton like both plants and animals?

Yes. The dinoflagellate is like a plant because it makes its own food. And it's like an animal because it swims, can see light and dark, and eats other plants and animals.

Some dinoflagellates actually produce brief flashes of light when disturbed. At night, you may see shallow water sparkle as you walk or paddle a boat through it. You're probably bothering a mass of dinoflagellates!

How many kinds of fish live in the ocean?

About 17,000 different kinds, or species. The smallest is the dwarf goby in the Indian Ocean. When full-grown it's less than one-half inch (1 cm) long. The largest fish is the whale shark. It swims in warm waters and can grow up to 60 feet (18 m) long!

Pilot fish

Which is the most numerous fish in the ocean?

The 3-inch (8 cm) bristlemouth. Experts say there are billions of bristlemouths swimming in the ocean.

What keeps most fish afloat?

A swim bladder. This organ is like a small balloon below the backbone. The swim bladder is filled with gas that fish produce in their blood. To stay afloat, a fish automatically keeps its bladder filled with the proper amount of gas.

Several kinds of fish—sharks, rays, tunas, dolphin fish, and those that live on the ocean bottom—have no swim bladders. But that's not a problem. Some sharks, for example, swallow air and use their stomachs as swim bladders. Other fish move rapidly up and down in the water. And bottom dwellers spend all their time on or near the ocean floor.

Carpet shark

Do all fish have bones?

Most, but not all. About 95 percent of fish, including tuna, trout, bass, cod, salmon, catfish, and thousands of others, have bony skeletons.

Others, like sharks and rays, have skeletons of cartilage. Cartilage is the strong but bendable material that gives shape to your nose and ears. Now you know why sharks and rays can twist and turn so easily in the water!

Are all sharks streamlined?

Not all. The hammerhead shark is a 15-foot-long (4.6 m) T-shaped creature with a 3-foot (0.9 m) bar across the front of its head. With eyes and nostrils at both ends of the bar, the shark can see or smell food coming and going.

The flat, wide carpet shark looks just like a rug on the ocean bottom. But don't be fooled. When a fish swims by, or someone steps on it, the shark flings open its big mouth and buries its razor-sharp teeth in the victim.

Hammerhead shark

How do fish breathe underwater?

Through gills, which are found just behind the head. Fish need to breathe oxygen, just as you do. But fish get their oxygen from water, not from air.

To breathe, a fish takes in water through its mouth and pumps it out over its gills. The gills remove oxygen from the water. Blood in the gills carries the oxygen all over the fish's body.

To stay alive, fish need a continual flow of water across their gills. Most have muscles that do the job automatically. Others, such as the tuna, must keep swimming without stopping in order to breathe.

Do fish sleep?

Yes, but not like you do. Many fish have times when they are less active than normal. Other fish swim continuously. During rest periods a fish's eyes stay open. The reason is simple. Most don't have eyelids!

Do fish make sounds?

Yes. Fish squeak, whistle, cough, snap, grind, slurp, or grunt. They make these sounds by vibrating their swim bladder or rubbing parts of their skeleton together.

The best-known fish sound comes from the gurnard fish. It grunts when a thunderstorm is coming. When fishermen hear this sound, they head for home!

Are fish warm-blooded or cold-blooded?

Cold-blooded. That means their temperature changes with variations in the water temperature. Fish are cold in cold water and warm in warm water. Fish in polar regions don't freeze because of a special chemical in their blood. The chemical lowers the freezing point of their blood and flesh, much like antifreeze in a car.

Close-up of a gill

Humpback whales

Harbor seals

Are whales fish?

No. Whales are mammals. Like you and other land mammals, whales breathe air and are warm-blooded. Their body temperature stays about the same, no matter how hot or cold the water. They also give birth to live young and raise them on milk from the mother's body.

How do whales breathe underwater?

They don't. Whales come up to the surface to breathe. When they dive, they hold their breath. A sperm whale dive can last up to two hours. When the whale comes up, it breathes out. The spout, or blow, looks like a fountain and can be seen from several miles (kilometers) away.

Do whales have teeth?

Most do. The sperm whale, the orca or killer whale, and about 60 other whales have teeth for catching fish and different sea animals—*not* for chewing.

   Other whales, including the gigantic blue whale and the gray whale, have no teeth. Instead they have long, fringed plates, called baleen, that hang from their upper jaw. These whales scoop up huge mouthfuls of water, which they then squeeze out with their tongue. Plankton in the water get stuck on the baleen and are swallowed by the whale. In one day, the blue whale gulps down about 4 tons (4 t) of plankton!

Do any sea mammals spend time on land?

Yes. Seals, sea lions, and walruses come out of the water when they are resting, mating, or giving birth. They spend the rest of the time in the ocean. Other sea mammals, such as whales, porpoises, and manatees, never leave the water.

What lives in the midzone of the ocean?

Animals, but no plants. Very little sunlight gets down to this zone, which reaches from 600 feet (180 m) to 3,000 feet (900 m) below the surface. Most of the fish here are small, seldom longer than 6 inches (15 cm).

At least one giant fish—the oarfish—swims in these midzone waters. Some grow to be as long as 50 feet (15 m). Few can overlook this odd creature with its snakelike body and bright red crest.

What is special about midzone fish?

Many make their own light! The light, which usually glows blue or green, comes from chemicals inside the bodies of the fish. It helps the fish attract prey, find mates, and surprise their enemies.

The hatchet fish is an example. It is a small, silvery fish shaped like a hatchet blade. Rows of tiny glowing lights line its belly. Some fish swim close to it to get a better look. Swiftly, the hatchet fish twists around, opens its huge mouth, and gulps down the unlucky prey!

How do midzone fish find food?

Several kinds of fish, like the hatchet fish and lantern fish, swim upward at night to hunt for their dinner. Special swim bladders let these fish rise as much as several hundred feet (meters) in search of food.

Which midzone fish has really long teeth?

The viper fish. The teeth are so long that they stay on the outside when the viper fish closes its mouth! And the teeth are so sharp and pointy that they can spear any fish that happens to swim by.

Lantern fish

Hatchet fish

Viper fish

Oarfish

What is it like on the deepest ocean floor?

Nasty. The temperature hovers near freezing, it's pitch-black, and the water pressure is more than 3 tons per square inch (3 t per 6.5 cm^2)!

How many animals live on the ocean bottom?

Only about 1 percent of all sea animals. But what a variety of bizarre-looking creatures they are!

The tripod fish, for example, is a walking fish! The three legs are its stiff tail and side fins.

The sea cucumber looks like a regular cucumber—but with short feet, called tube feet. When in danger, it squirts out long, sticky streamers that tangle up the enemy and let the sea cucumber escape.

Tube worms live on the ocean bottom in tall, thin tubes. They don't have to look for food. Bacteria in their body take in chemicals from the water and produce the food the tube worms eat.

Is there lots of food on the ocean bottom?

No. Food is hard to find, and it can be a long time between meals. When there is a lot to eat, the fish want to gulp down all they can. They have big mouths and stomachs that can expand to hold as much as they can swallow.

The gulper eel's jaws form a giant scoop. The mouth is by far the biggest part of its body. The fish swims slowly, with its jaws open, waiting for victims to swim in. Dozens of small, sharp teeth are ready to grab the prey.

The great swallower got its name from its huge mouth and elastic stomach. Only 6 inches (15 cm) long, it can swallow 10-inch-long (25 cm) fish. A big meal makes its stomach grow to many times its original size. The skin stretches so thin that you can actually see the food inside!

Do any deep-sea fish make their own light?

Yes. The anglerfish has a little rod sticking up from its head. It looks like a tiny fishing pole. At the end of the pole is a dangling blue-green light that attracts many fish. When one gets too close—ZAP!—the anglerfish gobbles it down!

The light of the flashlight fish comes from glowing bacteria in pouches under its eyes. The fish usually swims with the lights showing. But when threatened, it covers the light with an eyelid-like fold of skin. The flashlight fish darts away, leaving its enemy in the dark!

Scientists use powerful flashlights to see deep zone fish.

Gulper eel

Sea dragon

Anglerfish

Swallower

Tripod fish

Sea cucumber

Beard worms

Are there monsters at the bottom of the sea?

Yes—if you believe stories that sailors and others tell. Some legends are probably based on the giant squid. These beasts with their huge eyes and 10 flailing arms can grow as long as a big bus—about 60 feet (18 m)! Sometimes a giant squid rises to the surface. This enormous, weird-looking creature could easily be taken for a sea monster.

What is a mermaid?

A creature that is supposed to be half woman and half fish. Accounts of mermaids go back thousands of years. Today, experts say the mermaids sailors thought they saw were really manatees or dugongs. These sea mammals look human because they have smooth skin, and because one will sometimes poke straight up out of the water with its newborn held against its chest. But the animals also have big, flat tails, which is why they were thought to be half human and half fish.

Giant squid

ALONG THE COAST

What is a coast?

The land alongside the sea. While there are many types of coasts—from sandy beaches to rocky shores to muddy wetlands—they are all formed by the action of the sea.

How do beaches form?

Waves pound the coast. This grinds rocks and shells into tiny bits that become grains of sand. The waves drop the sand onto the shore to form the beaches.

Most sand grains are yellow or tan. The color comes mainly from rocks of a mineral called quartz. Some beaches are dazzling white. They're mostly made of tiny bits of coral or shell worn down by the sea. In the Hawaiian Islands the sand is black because it is made of ground-up volcanic lava.

What else builds up beaches?

Flowing rivers. They pick up and carry large amounts of soil from the banks and bottoms of riverbeds. When the rivers flow into the ocean, they drop this soil, which builds up into beaches.

How do rocky coasts form?

Either the land rises or the ocean level drops over millions of years. This leaves land that is much higher than the water. Ocean waves pick up sand, pebbles, and pieces of rock from the seafloor and hurl them against the shore. The wave action wears away the soil and breaks off pieces of rock. Over the years, the waves shape the land into cliffs and scatter immense boulders along the coastline.

How do muddy wetlands form?

The ocean covers a low-lying coastline with a shallow layer of water part or all the time. You usually find wetlands in protected bays or gulfs. The ground in the wetland is usually soft and muddy.

What good are wetlands?

Countless young sea creatures, including clams, crabs, and fish, begin life here. The water is calm, there are plenty of places to hide from enemies, and there's lots of food.

Wetlands are sometimes called "prairies of the sea" because of the many kinds of grasses that grow here and provide food for sea animals. Land animals, including foxes, deer, minks, and raccoons, also find food in wetlands. Some eat the grass; some eat the sea creatures.

Wetlands also help tame big storms and powerful waves. They protect inland farms, forests, and buildings, and stop the soil from washing away.

Mallard ducks

Great blue heron

Hermit crab

What plants are most common along ocean coasts?

Seaweeds. You can see seaweeds floating in ocean waters near coasts, attached to rocks and piers, and washed up on beaches.

All seaweeds are algae, which are not true plants. Algae make their own food as all plants do; but they lack the roots, stems, leaves, and flowers of true plants. The smallest seaweeds are the blue-green algae that sometimes form a slippery, slimy coating on shore rocks. The largest are kelp, which can grow to be 200 feet (61 m) long.

How do shore animals survive the changing tides?

Many hang on to rocks or fronds of seaweed. For example, mussels protect their soft bodies with hard shells. They tie themselves down to rocks with strong threads made of a sticky fluid from inside their body. Barnacles, on the other hand, attach themselves to an object with a cement-like material. There they stay for their entire life. During high tide, they open their shell at the top and kick out feathery feet to trap plankton. When the tide is out, barnacles close up tightly to keep from drying out.

Whitetail deer

Raccoon

What are tidal pools?

Rocky basins that often stay filled with water—even when the tide goes out. Various animals, such as hermit crabs, sea stars, and even some small fish, live in tidal pools.

Which animals live on sandy beaches?

Many different kinds. The beach may look empty of life—but don't believe it. Any number of animals, including clams, crabs, worms, and shrimp, live hidden just under the surface of the sand.

Razor clams have two long, thin, hard shells covering their soft body. Like other clams, they dig down into sandy beaches and feed on plankton that seep into the sand.

Some crabs hide out in sandy burrows or scurry along the beach and shallow water looking for food. Crabs have one pair of claws for grabbing food, and four pairs for walking. In some, the last pair is shaped like paddles for swimming.

Lugworms spend almost their entire life in the sand. They build an underground tube, open at the surface, and lie head down inside. Sand blown or washed into the little hole brings the lugworms the tiny bits of food they need to live.

Which fish lays eggs on the beach?

The grunion. On nights of the highest tides in spring and summer, these little fish ride waves onto beaches in California to lay and fertilize their eggs. What's amazing is that the males and females get the job done in about 30 seconds—in time to be carried back into the ocean by the very next wave. About two weeks later, incoming waves break open the eggs and sweep the newborn grunions out to sea!

Female sea turtles return to the beaches where they were born to lay their eggs. Then they leave. When the eggs hatch, the newborn turtles hurry into the water before birds or other animals can catch them.

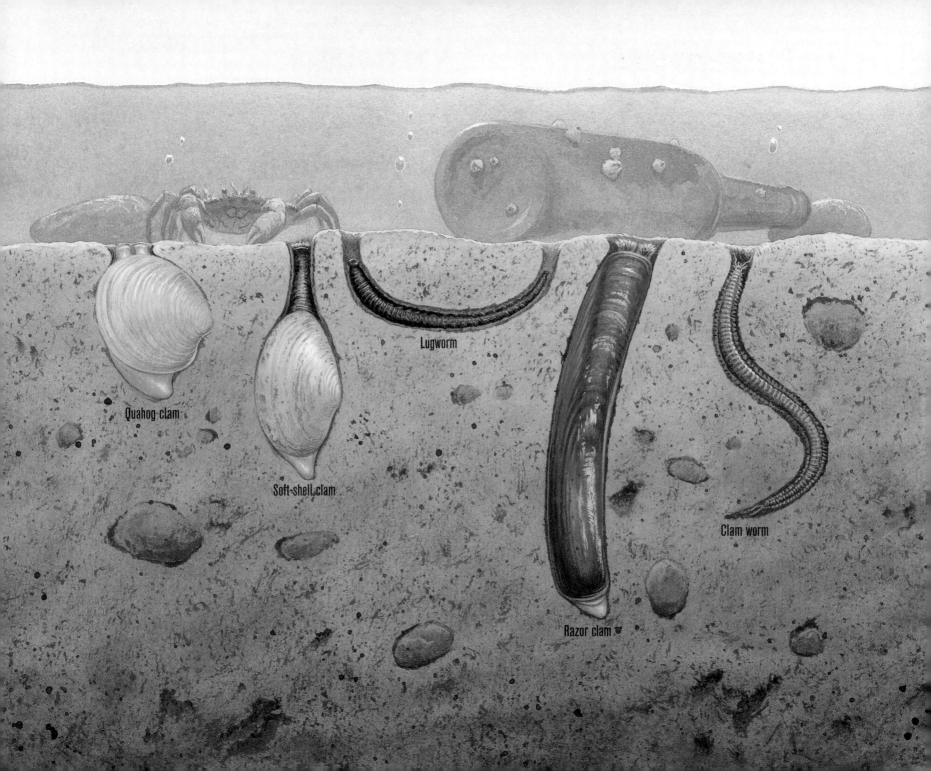

Quahog clam

Soft-shell clam

Lugworm

Razor clam

Clam worm

Northern gannet

Laughing gull

Common tern

Ring-billed gulls

23

Brown pelicans

Common tern

Double-crested cormorant

What are shorebirds?

Birds that live along the coast. All hunt in the sand, mud, or shallow waters for fish, clams, snails, worms, and other forms of life. And each has its own very special way of catching prey.

Sandpipers and sanderlings run after breaking waves, poking the sand with their bills to catch shellfish or worms. Terns also live along the shore, but are great divers. When a tern spots a fish, it plunges into the water headfirst, opens its beak, and nabs its prey.

What are seabirds?

Birds that spend most of their time over ocean waters sometimes far from land. Some, like the albatross, murre, and frigate bird, are fit for flying mile after mile (kilometer after kilometer) over long periods of time. Others, like the penguin, are not good flyers, but swim long distances, sometimes for months at a time.

Which bird is the deepest diver?

The emperor penguin. In 1990, an emperor penguin was measured at a depth of 1,584 feet (483 m). When a penguin dives, it can stay down as long as six minutes. You would be gasping for breath after only one minute!

Which seabird has the largest wingspan?

The wandering albatross. Its wingspan reaches more than 10 feet (3 m)—more than twice the distance from fingertip to fingertip when your arms are outstretched sideways. Small wonder the albatross can glide for hours over the ocean without flapping its wings once!

What is a coral reef?

A structure found in warm, shallow water around small islands and along the eastern shores of continents. Over thousands of years, the reefs build up from skeletons of millions of tiny animals called corals. Each reef looks like an amazing garden, with bright colors in all sorts of fantastic shapes—trees, fans, fingers, domes, and flowers.

The corals form hard, stony cups around themselves. They cement the cups together to become solid masses. As the corals die, they leave their skeletons behind. New colonies of corals grow on top of the old. In time, the huge masses of stony skeletons and living corals form reefs. Reefs may stretch for hundreds of miles (kilometers) and take thousands of years to build.

Which is the largest and best-known reef?

The Great Barrier Reef off the northeastern coast of Australia. It is more than 1,000 miles (1,600 km) long and has been built up over hundreds of millions of years.

Why are reefs important?

They're home to many, many sea creatures—from fish to worms. Animals find both food and shelter in reefs. The parrot fish, for example, scrapes and eats the coral. The moray eel hides in the reef during the day and hunts for prey at night.

Reefs also protect the coast. As big ocean waves strike the reef, they break and lose their energy. Without the protection of reefs, coastal areas would be more seriously damaged than they already are.

What keeps fish safe on the reef?

Camouflage. The blenny is a small fish with many enemies. When in danger, the blenny changes its spots, making it hard to see amid the coral. The Nassau grouper can change the pattern of its scales eight times in a few minutes to blend in with the reef colors!

Bar jacks

Crested blenny

Queen parrot fish

Queen angelfish

Clownfish

Anemone

Moray eel

Which reef animal looks like a flower?

The sea anemone (uh-NEM-uh-nee). But watch out for its long, thin "petals." They shoot out poisonous threads. Almost any small fish that swims near an anemone is a dead fish—except for the clownfish. The clownfish swims safely among the anemone's poisonous arms, protected by a slimy covering on its skin. In return, the clownfish helps to keep the anemone clean. Good work, partners!

Do coral reefs have any enemies?

People are a coral reef's worst enemy. Divers swim down to reefs and break off pieces of coral as souvenirs. Boaters drop anchors over reefs and smash the delicate coral. Also, many of us pollute coastal waters, which kills the growing coral.

Another danger to coral is the crown-of-thorns sea star, a huge animal that feeds on coral. These sea stars, which have multiplied greatly in recent years, have destroyed entire reefs.

What happens when a reef builds up above the water?

An island forms. Bits of broken coral and sand fill the openings in the reef to make it solid. Plant seeds and grains of soil from land blow out from shore and plants start to grow. Many of the islands in the Pacific Ocean are made of coral.

Why should you care about the ocean?

Because your life depends on it! The air you breathe, much of the food you eat, the rain that waters farmers' crops, and even your climate depend on the ocean. Life could not continue without the oceans of the world. So let's preserve and cherish our great natural treasure—and all that lives there!

INDEX

About the Authors

The Bergers have spent their entire lives at or close to the Atlantic Ocean. From their present home they can glimpse the ocean and take long walks along the shore. "We never tire of watching the waves and smelling the good ocean air," they say.

About the Illustrator

John Rice has always loved the simple pleasure of looking out to sea. Perhaps equally satisfying is the time he spends contemplating the wonderfully complex and beautiful world lying beneath the waves. He hopes that this book will show you a little of the magic that exists in the amazing world of nature.